THE ORIGINS AND PRACTICES OF YOGA: A WEENY INTRODUCTION

MATTHEW CLARK

MAHABONGO WEENY INTRODUCTIONS
VOL. 1

Cover illustration by Olivia Clifton-Bligh

Published by Lulu.com
4th Edition (2010)
Copyright © Matthew Clark

ISBN   978 -1 - 4461 - 9435 - 5

For further information or to order more copies of this book
e-mail: matt@mahabongo.com

Preface

The aim of this book is to provide for the non-specialist a very short and concise introduction to the origins and practices of yoga. Nearly all of the information presented may be found in other publications; some that I have found most useful have been included in the Bibliography. The positions that I have taken on particular topics, which are presented below, reflect my own personal conclusions; although the presentation has been distilled from two decades of both practising and researching yoga, particular points may need to be revised or corrected. Several friends and colleagues who are very knowledgeable in this field have kindly suggested some minor corrections, which have been incorporated in this edition.

Dr. Matthew Clark, Hove (September, 2010)
Post-Graduate Research Associate
School of Oriental and African Studies, University of London

This volume is the first in a series of Introductions to a variety of topics.

MAHABONGO WEENY INTRODUCTIONS

महाबोह्ने
MAHABONGO
麻葉 煩悩

Matthew Clark is also a musician, singer and song-writer:
www.mahabongo.com

Topics: Page:

1. Introduction

The term 'yoga' derives from the Sanskrit root *yuj*, meaning 'join', 'bind together' or 'harness' (such as of horses to a chariot). In the Indo-European family of languages, to which Sanskrit belongs, many cognate words may be found, such as 'yoke' in English. In the Indian context, yoga has several senses, and in this short article an attempt will be made to outline broadly what is known of its origins and practices. The focus is mainly on what has been termed 'postural' yoga, which involves work on the body. However, there are Hindu, Buddhist and Jain schools of yoga, and other derivative schools, for whom the main practice is meditation.

At its root, the practice of yoga is an attempt to transform the individual's consciousness through a variety of mental and practical techniques that work on the nervous system and brain chemistry. The yogi is essentially an experimenter with consciousness who may engage with various mental and physical disciplines and with regimens of particular kinds of plants or foods, modifying practice and consumption in order more easily to regulate the fluctuations of the mind. Yoga is a science, as the practitioner needs to observe and carefully analyse the effects of practice on his or her consciousness, health, well-being or psychic powers, and adopt or adjust to an attitude, lifestyle or behaviour which better contribute to the desired results. Historically, yogis have tended to live on the margins of society, experimenting with practices that generally run counter to traditional social norms and values.

In the long course of the development of mental science in South Asia, the term 'yoga' acquired several technical senses, one of them being a disciplined or controlled method. There is the element of discipline in all yogic practices, which is a vital component in the regulation of brain chemistry. Yoga might also be described as 'immersion': in psychic space or in an object of meditation. Deep states of immersion are perhaps best described as trance states, which may be experienced as a kind of 'suspension' of the normal world, or as a timeless union with something immeasurably larger than the individual practitioner. Such states are usually experienced, in one way or another, as an encounter with 'truth' or with ultimate or absolute 'reality', which are more vivid and profound than any experience in ordinary waking consciousness.

The ancient Sanskrit term *tapas* derives from the root *tap*, meaning 'heat'. *Tapas* also means austerities or asceticism, and is a feature of most yoga traditions. Rigorous yoga practices or the ingestion of psychedelic plants may result in an enormous sense of heat in the body, which can arise in trance states. Such supra-normal states can cause a cleaning of the biophysical system and be powerful aids to health. Perhaps obviously, the more radical the experiment with consciousness, the more the experimenter needs to be aware of the possible dangers and social difficulties that may result.

The practice of yoga is particularly associated with the Indian subcontinent. Some of the earliest reports available to us from travellers, such as from Greeks in the fourth century BCE, contain references to the practice of sometimes extreme asceticism by 'gymnosophists' attempting to gain wisdom. However, several of the techniques of yoga, including breath-control, meditation, the raising of heat in the body, and entry into near-death trance states, are not unique to South Asia. Similar or identical techniques have been employed for millennia by seekers of wisdom, health, immortality or occult power, in some shamanic traditions, in Taoism in China, and probably also in ancient Greek and Egyptian cultures.

2. Yoga in the Indus Valley civilization (2500–1500 BCE)

The earliest civilization of the Indian subcontinent was the so-called Indus Valley civilization, which flourished between 2500 and 1500 BCE. It had a sophisticated culture. Its people were proficient in shipbuilding, agriculture, metallurgy, and town planning. They had a writing system, which to date has not been deciphered. The script almost certainly does not record the spoken language. In 1921, under

3

the direction of Sir John Marshall, Director General of the Archaeological Survey of India, excavations properly began of the sites of the ruined cities of Mohenjo Daro (situated by the Indus river) and Harappa (situated by the Ravi river) in what is now Pakistan. During the last ninety years, archaeological finds have revealed the broad geographical extent of the civilization. Artefacts from the civilization have now been discovered at over a thousand sites, stretching from the Iranian border to south India, about 1,500 kilometres from the initial excavations.

Concerning the origins of yoga, one of the most discussed archaeological finds from the Indus culture is what is usually referred to as the 'proto-Shiva' seal (of which there are a number of examples) made of steatite, which depicts a figure seated in what looks like a yoga posture, wearing a head dress with curved horns, and in some examples, surrounded by several kinds of animals. Sir John Marshall believed that this image could be a representation of a form of Shiva (one of the main deities of Hinduism) seated in a yoga posture in his aspect as Pashupati, meaning 'Lord of the Animals'; another of Shiva's aspects is as the Lord of Yoga (Yogishvara). For decades, scholars argued whether or not the seal provided enough information or detail to make an unequivocal identification with either yoga or with a form of Shiva. Thomas McEvilley (**1**) maintains that the seal probably does represent someone doing a yoga posture; and that the figure may be a 'shamanic' proto-Shiva. Several scholars have suggested that there is an ancient stream of yoga that has persisted in South Asia since before any kinds of records began, while others argue that the only clear evidence for the physical practices of yoga date from a much later period, perhaps around the middle of the first millennium BCE.

3. Yoga in the Vedas (1500–800 BCE)

Waves of migration of people from what is now southern Russia who called themselves 'Arya' (meaning 'noble') first reached South Asia some time after the demise of the Indus Valley culture, between 1900 and 1500 BCE. These people rode horses, were nomadic for many centuries, and kept cattle. They did not construct buildings, only makeshift shelters. At the centre of their cultural life was the performance of ritual ceremonies around fireplaces. Domestic ceremonies were performed daily, while ceremonies known as 'sacrifices' that sometimes lasted several days were periodically performed. Classes of priests (who became known as Brahmans) from particular families very exactly chanted and recited holy, oral texts known as *Veda*, which gradually enlarged with the incorporation of new hymns, reaching its final form (as four texts) around 800 BCE. Other texts, including the *Upanishads* were added subsequently.

In the *Vedas* there is no concept of metaphysical *karma* or of reincarnation or rebirth (though some notions of this idea may be found): after death one went either to the land of the gods or to the land of the fathers. The concepts of metaphysical *karma* and reincarnation only began appearing in Brahmanical culture after about 800 BCE. The gods of Vedic culture were typically invoked for long life, health, children (particularly sons), and victory in battle against their enemies. Among the main gods, to whom the bulk of Vedic hymns were addressed, were Agni (god of fire), Indra (chief of the gods) and Soma (who is also both an intoxicating drink and a plant). The identity of Soma has been discussed for many decades by scholars. However, arguably, based on textual references, Soma was prepared from a mixture of two plants, which resulted in a form of *ayahuasca*, a very powerful psychedelic potion. There is evidence of its use in South America since the early centuries BCE by indigenous Indians. Since the 1920s, several South American Christian churches have been established that use *ayahuasca* in their ceremonies.

In the ritual texts of *Vedas*, the term *yoga* occurs, but in a merely prosaic sense referring, for example, to the yoking of horses to wagons; there is no occurrence in the *Veda* of the term being used in the sense of a spiritual discipline. Between around 800 BCE and 200 CE, another class of texts known as *Upanishads* were composed; twelve (or thirteen) *Upanishads* (which are usually referred to as the 'classical' *Upanishads*) were subsequently appended to one or another of the four *Vedas*. These texts, although incorporated as a part of the *Veda*, are not texts used for ritual; they are partly poetic and have a philosophical component: questions, for example, about the destiny of the soul, about liberation, or about the end of suffering, are often framed in the form of dialogues between a sage or a Brahman and a king.

4. Yoga in the Upanishads (800 BCE–200 CE), Buddhism and Jainism

Perhaps the earliest textual references to *yoga* as a spiritual discipline occur around 600/500 BCE in the *Taittiriya Upanishad*: *yogatma* (II.4.1) refers to an inner self which is made of knowledge and which is *yoga*; and *yogakshema* (III.10.2) refers to 'getting and enjoying' in the breath and the lower breath. In the *Katha Upanishad*, which was probably composed between 300 and 100 BCE, are the first explicit references to yoga, which is referred to as *adhyatmayoga* (the yoga of the self): "By the study of the yoga of the self, the wise one knows as god that which is hard to see, that is deeply hidden" (II.12); "The steadfast control of the senses is known as 'yoga'; then one becomes undistracted; for yoga is the origin and the passing away" (VI.11); "The senses of the one without understanding, with mind ever undisciplined, are out of control, like evil horses of a charioteer" (III.5) (**2**). Further references to yoga occur in later classical *Upanishads*, notably in the *Shvetashvatara* and *Maitri Upanishads* (dating from the early centuries BCE), where the concepts of withdrawing the senses, controlling the mind, and attaining liberation were further elaborated.

The practices and physiology of yoga were also explained in other, later collections of *Upanishads*, notably in the *Yoga*

*Upanishad*s, a corpus of about twenty-two texts that are orientated to Vedanta philosophy, and which reached its final compilation in the eighteenth century, comprising some rewritings of older texts and several newly composed texts. In these texts several forms of yoga are elaborated, including *mantra yoga*, *laya yoga* (which dissolves mental activity), *hatha yoga* (which has eight degrees, roughly corresponding to the eight limbs of Patanjali's system: see below), and *raja yoga*, which is identified with *hatha yoga* in some of the *Yoga Upanishad*s.

Beginning around 500 BCE, new sects arose on the subcontinent; some disappeared, but Buddhism and Jainism flourished and had a great impact on Indian culture and thinking. In Buddhism, yoga means specifically meditation (or meditative techniques), while in Jainism, there is also an ancient tradition of yoga practices, primarily involving austerities and meditation techniques. In some schools of Buddhism and Jainism visualisations and the chanting of *mantra*s are also performed. Jain yoga also incorporates some of the technical vocabulary of Patanjali (see Section 6).

5. Yoga in the Bhagavad Gita (c. 100 CE)

The popular text of the *Bhagavad Gita*, which is in eighteen chapters, comprises about two-thirds of *The Book of the Bhagavad Gita* (*Bhagavadgitaparvan*), which is the sixty-third of the hundred minor books of the *Mahabharata*. The *Mahabharata* was composed from bardic and local sources between about 500 BCE and 400 CE; it is a massive text (the longest epic in the world) of around 100,000 verses, and is by far the largest of the two great epics of Hinduism (the other being the *Ramayana*). In the *Mokshadharma* section of the *Mahabharata*, which is a part (chapters 168–353) of the twelfth major book (*Shantiparvan*), various philosophical schools are discussed, including that of yoga.

In the *Bhagavad Gita*, Arjuna is given divine instruction by his charioteer, who is the god Krishna in disguise. The setting for the instruction is a battlefield (at Kurukshetra, near Delhi) upon which two branches of the Bharata (or Kuru) family, to which Arjuna belongs, are about to go to war. Krishna instructs Arjuna that there are three kinds of yoga: *jnana yoga* (the yoga of knowledge), *bhakti yoga* (the yoga of religious devotion), and *karma yoga* (the yoga of action without a desire for reward). These three paths are essentially 'mental' paths, none of which requires discipline of the body or of the breath. In the *Bhagavad Gita*, yoga is nearly always for some purpose, requiring strenuous effort, which transforms the 'vision' and understanding of the practitioner. The *Gita* warns against withdrawal from the world: liberation results from spiritual insight, devotion to god, or from selflessly performing our social duties, knowing that our souls undergo transmigration in many bodies over many aeons.

6. The eight-limbed yoga system of Patanjali (c. 250 CE)

The best-known text on yoga is the *Yoga Sutra* of Patanjali, in which is to be found the *ashtanga* ('eight-subsidiary'/'eight-limbed') *yoga* system. The *Yoga Sutra* has 195 verses, which are divided into four sections (*padas*). About 1500 CE, a system of six orthodox, philosophical views (*darshanas*) was formulated by Brahmans; the yoga system was included, paired with the Samkhya system of philosophy, which essentially posits a fundamental distinction between what might be called the constituents of consciousness (which includes the external world), and a faculty of pure awareness that observes those constituents. It should be emphasized that in the Indian philosophical tradition, maintaining a particular philosophy was traditionally not a merely abstract exercise: it also entailed adopting a particular way of life associated with the system, which included specific rules of diet and dress.

The *Yoga Sutra* is believed to have been composed around 250 CE, and is traditionally studied with the most important of its commentaries, the *Yoga Sutra Bhashya* of Vyasa (c. 500/600 CE). Other influential commentaries were written by Vacaspati Mishra (c.

850 CE), King Bhoja (c. 1050 CE), and Vijnana Bhikshu (c. 1550 CE). Pantanjali was possibly not the author of the *Yoga Sutra*, but may perhaps have been a compiler of popular aphorisms on yoga. It is only in the tenth century CE that the *Yoga Sutra* is first attributed to Patanjali **(3)**. Very little is known about Patanjali. Almost certainly another Patanjali (c. 250 BCE) composed a work on grammar; and another Patanjali was the author in probably the eleventh century of manuals of temple ritual at the south Indian Nataraja temple at Chidambaram.

Although Patanjali's *ashtanga yoga* system is sometimes equated with *raja yoga* ('royal'/'best' yoga), the term *raja yoga* does not appear in the *Yoga Sutra*. Some scholars believe that the section in the *Yoga Sutra* detailing the eight limbs (II.29) could be a quotation or a later interpolation into the original text **(4)**. It is possible that the *Yoga Sutra* was originally a commentary on a six-limbed yoga system, which is common to both Brahmanical and Tantric Buddhist traditions. Most of the six-limbed systems lack the first three *anga*s (*yama, niyama, asana*), and introduce *tarka* ('reason'/'logic') in Brahmanical systems, or *anusmrti* ('remember'/'recollect') in the Buddhist Tantras **(5)**. However, the *Yoga Sutra* that has come down to us presents a coherent and integrated system that presents a defined path of practice.

At II.29 in the *sutra*, Patanjali lists the eight limbs: "*yama-niyama-asana-pranayama-pratyahara-dharana-dhyana-samadhi...*".
External limbs: 1. *yama* ('restraints'), 2. *niyama* ('observances'),

   3. *asana* ('posture'), 4. *pranayama* ('breath control'),

   5. *pratyahara* ('withdrawal of senses').
Internal limbs: [= *samyama yoga* ('yoga of self-control')]:

   6. *dharana* ('concentration on an object'),

   7. *dhyana* ('meditation'), 8. *samadhi* ('trance').

(See Appendix for a summary of the main concepts of the *Yoga Sutra*.)

Patanjali defines yoga in the second verse of the *sutra*: "Yoga is the cessation of the *vrtti*s ('fluctuations'/'turnings'/'modifications') of the mind". By practising what amounts to moral virtues (*yamas* and *niyamas*) as a prerequisite, restraining the senses (*pratyahara*), and by sitting still and comfortably, which assists control (and, ultimately, stopping *nirodha*) of the breath (*pranayama*), mental activity may cease, eventually resulting in the uncovering of the shining of the inner light and *samadhi* (which might be best translated as 'trance' or 'enstasy'); this may lead to liberation, which Patanjali calls *kaivalya* ('alone-ness'). One-pointed concentration (*ekagrata*) can eliminate the distractions of consciousness, caused by sense impressions and unconscious influences from the previously acquired or inherited tendencies (*samskaras*) of consciousness. Patanjali defines *kriya yoga* (II.1) as comprising asceticism (*tapas*), study on one's own (*svādhyāya*), and devotion to the Lord (*ishvarapranidana*).

Two significant features of the *Yoga Sutra* may be noted. Firstly, although *asana* ('posture') is one of eight limbs of Patanjali's system, the term *asana* only occurs twice in the *sutra*: at II.29, in a list of the eight limbs; and then at II.46, where there is a comment that *asana* should be 'steady and comfortable' (*sthira-sukham-asanam*). (Also in the classical *Upanishads*, *asana* does not feature as a yogic practice.) Although the *Yoga Sutra* does not mention postures, Vyasa, in the earliest available commentary (c. 500–700 CE) on the *Yoga Sutra*, lists eleven postures that may aid sitting steadily and comfortably.

Secondly, about a quarter of the *Yoga Sutra* is devoted to *siddhi*s ('attainments') or *vibhuti*s ('supernatural powers'). The third section of the *Yoga Sutra* (the *Vibhuti Pada*) summarises the *vibhuti*s, which include, amongst others: knowledge of previous births (III.18); knowledge of another's consciousness (III.19); invisibility (III.21); knowledge of the world, the sun, the stars and their movement of planets (III.26–28); the non-adhesion to water, mud or thorns (III.39); traversing the ether (III.42); mastery over the elements (III.44); and the perfection of the body and the indestructibility of its constituents

(III.45). Supernatural powers are not necessarily a distraction from the practice of yoga, but are a by-product of it. At III. 37, Patanjali says: "In *samadhi* these [supernatural] powers are epiphenomena (or, possibly, obstacles, *upasargas*) in ordinary awareness". However, in this remark, Patanjali is not referring to all of the powers, but only to the experiences mentioned in the two previous verses: knowledge of the self, and flashes of sensory illumination. Patanjali also states (IV.1) that supernatural powers may be the result of birth, [ingesting] herbs, mantra-recitation, asceticism or enstasy (trance).

7. Textual references to the practice of yoga postures (1450–1800 CE)

As noted in Section 2, it seems probable that yoga postures were known and practised in South Asia in the second or third millennium BCE, though the evidence is very slight; and it is likely that there has since been a continuous though largely unrecorded tradition of practice among the itinerant yogis of the Indian subcontinent. Besides Vyasa's mention of postures (referred to in Section 6), slightly later evidence for the practice of yoga postures dates from the eighth/ninth century CE, when stone carvings around temples were made in south India depicting yogis with large earrings in a number of yoga postures. Also in the eighth/ninth century, Tirumular, a Tamil *siddha*, in his *Tirumantiram* lists eight postures out of what he says are 180 postures.

The *Pashupata Sutra*, which dates from the around 300 CE, describes the yoga practice of a radical sect of yogis, the Pashupatas, who were almost identical in lifestyle with the Greek cynics. They lived on the margins of society, in caves, cremation grounds and remote places, covering themselves with ashes, shunning society, sometimes acting crazily, insulting people and getting insulted, practising *pranayama* and attaining yoga and supernatural powers. (However, by the end of the first millennium CE, the Pashupatas had many monasteries in several countries in Asia, and exerted considerable political influence.) The Pashupatas were similar in many ways to *aghoris*, the most radical branch of a sect of yogis called Nath (meaning 'Lord'), Nath-Siddha, or Kanphata ('split ear', from their large earrings), who are still numerous in India and Nepal.

According to tradition, the Naths were organized into twelve branches by Gorakhnath (or Gorakshnath), who may have lived in the twelfth century. Gorakhnath's guru was Matsyendranath, who appears in many contexts in South Asian religions, particularly in connection with the transmission of esoteric Tantric texts. Matsyendranath is also the patron saint of Nepal. Gorakhnath and Matsyendranath are members of a group of nine Naths, a still-popular South Asian tradition (particularly among the lower classes), who are wonder-working magicians and yogis.

Attributed to Naths are a few dozen texts that describe yoga practices and physiology that do not feature in the treatment of yoga by Patanjali. (However, recent work (2010) by James Mallinson indicates that Naths may not have authored many of the texts that are attributed to them.) Perhaps the earliest Sanskrit text on *hatha yoga* is the *Gorakshashataka* ('The hundred verses of Gorakshnath'), composed around 1400 CE, which mentions two yoga postures (*padmasana* and *vajrasana*), four kinds of *pranayama*, the *mula, uddiyana* and *jaladhara bandhas*, and the arousing of *kundalini*. *'Hatha'* means 'force' or 'exertion', and *hatha yoga* generally refers to strenuous physical exercises involving postures, controlled breathing (*pranayama*), and body-cleaning practices for the purification of *nadis* (though in some texts *hatha yoga* only refers to *pranayama*).

Besides the *Yoga Sutra*, one of the best-known texts on yoga is the *Hatha Yoga Pradipika* ('An explanation of Hatha Yoga') of Svatmarama, compiled in the fifteenth century, which contains twenty-eight verses from the original text of the *Gorakshashataka*. Near the beginning of the *Hatha Yoga Pradipika* (v. 5), Shiva, Matysyendra and Goraksha are included in a list of teachers who have conquered death through the practice of *hatha yoga*, which is said to be the ladder to the heights of *raja yoga*. In the *Hatha Yoga Pradipika*, fifteen yoga postures are mentioned. Besides the *Hatha Yoga Pradipika* and *Gorakshashataka*, perhaps the two best-known yoga texts, which are also attributed to Naths, are the *Shiva Samhita* (c. 1400 CE), and the *Gheranda Samhita* (c. 1700 CE), wherein are described, respectively, four and thirty-three postures. According to the *Shiva Samhita*, eighty-four *asana*s were taught by Shiva; according to the *Gheranda Samhita*, 8,400,000 *asana*s. In nearly all texts, the most important *asana* is *padmasana*, the 'lotus posture'.

8.   Physiology and practices in Nath yoga texts
In the yoga texts attributed to Naths, obstacles to yoga (such as overeating), rules of conduct (*yama*s and *niyama*s) are explained, as are prohibitions on associating with women and on particular kinds of food. There are descriptions of yoga postures, breathing exercises, body-cleaning practices, and Tantric physiology that employs the concepts of *chakra*s, *granthi*s and *nadi*s.

Chakras are psycho-physical 'wheels' that are located inconsistently (depending on which text is referred to) in various places in the body (usually six in the body and one just above the crown *chakra*, on top of the head). Details of the *chakra*s do not feature prominently in most yoga texts. However, in many Tantric works more detail is supplied. *Chakra*s are also referred to as *mandala*s and as lotus flowers, each with a different number of petals (or 'spokes'), which are the seats of deities, both male and female. The fifty-two phonemes of the Sanskrit alphabet are known as *bija* ('seed') *mantra*s, each corresponding to a deity, which are distributed amongst the petals of the lotuses. Associated with each *chakra* are particular colours, elements and also geometric figures (with their own colour). Also described in many works on Tantra is the iconography of deities and further details of their associated animals (their vehicles).

In some texts, up to fourteen 'knots' (*granthi*s) are described. In the rising of *kundalini*, these knots may be pierced. In the *Hatha Yoga Pradipika* three *granthi*s are mentioned as important: *brahma granthi*, in the chest; *vishnu granthi*, in the throat; and *rudra granthi*, between the eyebrows. However, other texts refer to two important *granthi*s: in the genital area and between the eyebrows.

Throughout the body are *nadi*s (72,000 in some texts), which are psycho-physical 'streams' or 'channels', the most important of them being the *ida* (on the left side, connected with the left nostril), *sushumna* (the central channel) and *pingala* (on the right side, connected with the right nostril). These three *nadi*s pass from an area near the base of the spine to the cranium. According to the *Dhyanabindu Upanishad*, which is one of the *Yoga Upanishad*s, ten *nadi*s are important for breath circulation.

The usually dormant female 'snake' (*kundalini*) lies coiled eight times near the base of the spine, and when aroused she travels up the central (*sushumna*) spinal channel, piercing the *chakra*s, to the cranium, where she unites with the male energy, resulting in an ecstatic experience of drops of nectar dripping into one's head. An experience also referred to is of the 'unstruck sound' (*anahata* or *shabda brahma*), which occurs when the *kundalini* reaches the heart *chakra*. The *kundalini*, in her ascent and descent, from *chakra* to *chakra*, reabsorbs the elements of the microcosm (the *tattvas*), which had been brought into manifestation in the 'unfolding' of the universe in its corporeal forms. This is why the yogi who masters the *kundalini* is the 'Lord of the Universe'.

Attaining bliss, immortality, control of one's own psycho-physical processes and of the natural world, and liberation while alive (*jivanmukti*) are the goals of these practices.

9. Cleansing techniques

In the yoga texts attributed to Naths, besides yoga postures, related yoga exercises of internal cleansing and purification are discussed. In the résumé below, it needs to be noted that texts are not entirely consistent regarding the names and kinds of yogic practices. One group of cleansing techniques described in the *Hatha Yoga Pradipika* is the 'six actions' (*shat karmans*), which are also referred to as *kriya*s (the list varies slightly in other texts):

1. *dhauti* (of which there are four kinds: internal, teeth, heart, rectum; which involve cleaning the mouth, stomach and intestinal tract with cloth and water to remove accumulated impurities);
2. *basti* (enema);
3. *neti* (passing water or cloth through the nasal passages);
4. *trataka* (staring fixedly at a light source to allow water to clean the eyes);
5. *nauli* (a contraction and rotation of the abdominal muscles);
6. *kapalabati* (rapid inhalation and exhalation).

10. Breath control (*pranayama*)

Breath control (*pranayama*), of various kinds, is important in almost all systems of yoga. In the Nath texts, several techniques are described; they are practised for related purposes: to 'cleanse' the psycho-physical system, including particular *nadi*s; and to direct vital energy in the body into the central *sushumna nadi* (near the spine) so that it may activate the rising of *kundalini*. Among the various regimens and types of *pranayama* discussed are: *bhastrika* (rapidly and forcefully expelling air from the nose); *surya bhedana* (drawing air in through the right nostril and expelling it through the left nostril); *shitali* (drawing air in through a curled tongue, to cool the body); *ujjayi* (breathing with the throat slightly contracted); *khumbaka* (forceful retention of breath; up to eight kinds of this exercise are mentioned); *puraka* (inhaling and retaining breath through alternate nostrils); and *rechaka* (prolonged expulsion of breath). It is sometimes recommended that *pranayama* be accompanied by visualizations of deities and the recitation of mantras. Some exercises are performed when one is partially submerged in water.

Pranayama also enables the regulation of the 'breaths' that reside in the body. The chief breath, *prana*, appears in the *Brhadaranyaka* and *Chandogya Upanishads*; it denotes ordinary breath and the life-force. Other 'breaths' appear in later texts and also in Ayurvedic texts. In the *Upanishads*, although not always clear, there is an identification of *prana* with breathing out, *apana* with breathing in, *udana* with breath moving up, *vyana* with the breath that traverses, *samana* with the breath that equalizes or links.

According to Nath texts, five major and five minor breaths are explained. In the *Gorakshashataka* the five major breaths are as follows:

1. *prana* is seated in the heart and is the breath;
2. *apana* is situated in the lower trunk, seated in the rectum, and regulates urination and excretion;
3. *samana* resides in the navel and governs the function of digestion;
4. *udana* lies in the middle of the throat and governs the function of speech;
5. *vyana* pervades the whole body.

The five minor breaths are:

1. *naga*, which causes eructation;
2. *kurma*, which functions in winking;
3. *krkara*, causing sneezing or hunger;
4. *revadatta*, causing yawning;
5. *dhananjaya*, which is the breath that remains in the body after death.

11. Internal psycho-physical techniques

Another feature of Nath yoga physiology are the three *bandhas*, the muscle contractions or 'locks' that facilitate the containment and regulation of psychic energy within the body. They are used particularly as an adjunct to breathing exercises. The three *bandhas* are the *mulabandha* (situated just above the anal and genital muscles), the *uddiyanabandha* (just below the diaphragm), and the *jalandharabandha* (the throat lock).

Many *mudra*s (which means 'seal', 'stamp' or 'impression') are also described (twenty-five in the *Gheranda Samhita*). Particular *mudra*s entail specific kinds of *pranayama* and *bhanda*s, while some require a posture, most commonly *padmasana* ('lotus position'). Three of the *mudra*s are the three *bandha*s (described above); other *mudra*s are particular kinds of concentration (such as on an external object or the tip of the nose), maintaining a shoulder stand (*viparitakarani*), *shanmukhi mudra* (closing the ears, nose and eyes with the fingers), *vajroli mudra* (which involves drawing up liquid into the penis), and *khechari mudra* (the 'flying' *mudra*), which entails rolling the tongue back to allow the tip to seal the nasal passage and release nectar from the cranial vault.

12. Yoga in the West in the twentieth century: various schools

(i) The influence of Svami Vivekananda
Apart from academic specialists, few people outside Asia knew about yoga until the 1950s. Probably the most influential person initially to draw attention in the West to yoga was Svami Vivekananda (1863–1902), the main disciple of Paramahamsa Ramakrishna (1836–1886), a Bengali Tantric and mystic. As a representative of the Hindu religion, Vivekananda travelled from India to the USA to attend the Parliament of Religions at Chicago in 1893, where he delivered lectures on Hinduism. He subsequently lectured in other cities in the USA, in England and in Europe, attracting worldwide press-coverage. Vivekananda's book *Raja Yoga* was published in 1896, introducing readers to his interpretation of yoga, which in some respects differed from how yoga had been traditionally understood in India. Vivekananda emphasised spiritual experience as the most important

17

component of religion, maintaining that the 'universal truth' of Hinduism was grounded in experience and not in dogma. He has been credited with the coining of the idea of the 'materialistic West' and the 'spiritual East'. During his lecture tours, Vivekanadanda initiated the establishment of what was to become a worldwide network of ashrams, the Ramakrishna Mission in India, and the Vedanta Society in the West.

(ii) The influence of Krishnamacharya

The most important influence on the diffusion of yoga in the West in the twentieth century was Tirumulai Krishnamacharya (1888–1989) who was from south India. During his lifetime, Krishnamacharya had many students, the best-known being B. K. S. Iyengar, Patabhi Jois, Krishnamacharya's son T. K. V. Desikachar, and Indra Devi. Other influential students were A. G. Mohan and Srivasta Ramaswamy. Probably, about eighty percent of the yoga practised in the West is connected directly or indirectly with the lineage of Krishnamacharya, the largest movement being Iyengar Yoga, followed by Ashtanga Yoga (taught by Patabhi Jois), and then Viniyoga (taught by Desikachar).

Besides being a yogi, Krishnamacharya was a scholar who held degrees in various branches of Indian philosophy from six Indian universities; he also wrote many books in several languages. He was also accomplished in temple and household rituals. As a young boy, Krishnamacharya was first taught yoga by his father. He learned twenty-four yoga postures from the Shankaracharya of Sringeri, became a Sanskrit and philosophy teacher, and taught yoga to some of his students. In 1919, he travelled to Tibet to study yoga with Ramamohan Brahmachari, who lived in a cave near Mount Kailash. Krishnamacharya stayed for seven years with Ramamohan Brahmachari, who became his guru. Krishnamacharya studied yoga texts, *asana* and *pranayama*, and furthered his knowledge of the healing applications of yoga practices. Until the end of his life,

Krishnamacharya continued teaching and studying philosophy and Ayurveda. He was renowned as a healer, possessing not only extensive knowledge of therapeutic yoga practices, but also of curative plants and nutrition. It is claimed that he was able to stop the pulse of his heart for two minutes.

In 1925 Krishnamacharya got married to Namagiriammal; then, in 1931, at the invitation of the Maharaja of Mysore, Krishna Rajendra Wodeyar, Krishnamacharya became the resident yoga teacher at the Mysore palace. He organized postures into groups and sequences, linking practice to rhythmic breathing. Krishnamacharya was particularly influential in introducing 'postural' *hatha* yoga to the West, not as a practice that is necessarily a preliminary to meditation, but as an adjunct to it. The widespread diffusion in India of Western gymnastic routines, beginning around the end of the nineteenth century, seems to have significantly influenced the development of yoga routines at the Mysore palace.

(iii) B. K. S. Iyengar and Hatha Yoga
In Britain, the two most influential schools of 'postural' yoga are Iyengar Yoga and the British Wheel of Yoga, which was founded in 1962. Besides teaching its own courses, the British Wheel of Yoga also acts as an umbrella organization, validating the training programmes of an increasing number of other British yoga groups, including Viniyoga and the Scottish Yoga Teachers Association.

The Iyengar Yoga system is also called Hatha Yoga. B. K. S. Iyengar (b. 1918) learned yoga from Krishnamacharya, who was his brother-in-law. Although Iyengar stayed with Krishnamacharya from 1934 to 1937, he only studied yoga with him for ten or fifteen days during that time. Iyengar then moved to Pune, became a professional yoga teacher and established the Iyengar Yoga Institute. He says that although he was not taught for very long by Krishnamacharya, those lessons determined what he has become today.

An important influence on general public awareness of yoga was the violinist Yehudi Menuhin, who was instrumental in introducing his yoga teacher Iyengar to Europe, for the first time in 1954. Iyengar also went to the USA in 1956. In 1960, at the invitation of Yehudi Menuhin, Iyengar came to London to teach a small group of yoga students, returning every year to teach an ever-increasing number of them. Iyengar's book *Light on Yoga*, first published in 1966, became a standard English-language work for yoga practitioners. The Iyengar Yoga school is still growing worldwide, teaching the system and philosophy of Hatha Yoga, which places considerable emphasis on the correct practice of *asana*s, and also teaches meditation and *pranayama*.

During the last fifty years, many former students of Iyengar have branched out and devised either their own systems of yoga, or have adapted Iyengar Yoga.

(iv) Patabhi Jois and Ashtanga Yoga

Besides teaching Iyengar, Krishnamacharya also taught Patabhi Jois (1915–2009). Patabhi Jois' system is called Ashtanga Yoga (and also Vinyasa Yoga: *vinyasa* means 'arrangement'), which has significantly gained in popularity in the West since the early 1990s. Patabhi Jois started learning yoga from Krishnamacharya in 1927, and continued as his student for twenty-five years. From 1937, Jois began teaching at the Sanskrit College in Mysore, and in 1948 established the Ashtanga Yoga Research Institute. In 1964, Jois' photograph and address appeared in the book *Pranayama* by the Belgian author André van Lyspeth. Jois only taught family members and young men from the local community in Mysore until the early 1970s, when he began teaching foreign students. Jois first taught yoga abroad in California in 1975.

Jois' system is one of the most energetic and aerobic styles of yoga. Groups of postures are arranged in six series, with three levels of increasing difficulty. Emphasised are rhythmic breathing during the practice, the raising of heat in the body, and the application of 'locks' (*bandhas*) in postures. *Pranayama* is also taught, usually after mastery of the 'Primary Series', the first level of postures. Several styles of yoga are derivative, to a greater or lesser degree, of Jois' system; among the best-known are Bikram Yoga and Power Yoga.

Jois' system is known as Astanga Yoga, which occasionally leads to some misunderstanding among yoga students. As noted in Section 6, Patanjali's eight-limbed (*ashtanga*) system only twice briefly mentions *asana* ('posture'): no postures are presented. (However, as also mentioned, Vyasa, the commentator on the *Yoga Sutra*, lists eleven postures for sitting steadily and comfortably.) Jois inherited the philosophical tradition of Ashtanga Yoga from his guru, Krishnamacharya, but Krishnamacharya taught a system of lengthy sequences of postures, incorporating *bandhas*. He devised a system that incorporated what are essentially Nath yoga practices, but omitted some of the most radical exercises, such as *vajroli mudra*. So, even though the philosophy of Ashtanga Yoga is in the tradition of Patanjali, the practices are not based on Patanjali's *Yoga Sutra*.

(v) Desikachar and Viniyoga
Another of Krishnamacharya's students was his son T. K. V. Desikachar, who studied with his father for twenty-nine years, learning religious rituals, all aspects of yoga, and the traditional branches of Indian philosophy. Viniyoga (which could be translated as 'applied yoga') aims to tailor particular practices of yoga to suit individual needs. The main branches of the school are in Chennai and California. In general, besides the teaching of *asanas*, *bandhas*, and *pranayama*, there is more practice of chanting and devotional rituals in Viniyoga than in the other schools in the lineage of Krishnamacharya. Owing to the occasional misinterpretation of the name 'Viniyoga', Desikachar suggested the renaming of his system. In Britain, since 2004, the Viniyoga school has been called the Association for Yoga Studies.

(vi) Indra Devi

Born in Riga (Latvia) as Eugenie Peterson (1899–2002), Indra Devi (as she became known) was an early disciple of Krishnamacharya and became an internationally renowned yoga teacher. She moved to Argentina in 1982, and was elected president of honour of the International Yoga Federation and the Latin American Union of Yoga. One of Indra Devi's students, Richard Hittleman, became well known in the 1970s through his TV appearances in the USA.

(vii) Sivananda Yoga

Besides the schools that derive from the lineage of Krishnamacharya, probably the two next most influential are the Sivananda and Bihar schools of yoga. Sivananda took initiation as a *samnyasi* in 1924 from Svami Vishvanandasarasvati, and subsequently founded the Divine Life Society in 1936 in Haridvar. The organisation grew over the subsequent decades to become internationally established, with centres running training programmes in several countries. Besides the study of *asana, pranayama*, meditation and Hindu scriptures, a notable feature of Sivanada yoga courses is the singing and chanting of devotional, religious songs. The Sivananda organization has published many books by Sivananda and has charitable and educational programmes in India.

(viii) Satyananda Yoga (Bihar School of Yoga)

The Bihar School of Yoga and the International Yoga Fellowship were founded in 1964 by Paramahamsa Satyananda Sarasvati (1923–2009). Aged nineteen, Satyananda took *samnyasa* ('renunciation') initiation from Svami Sivananda at the Sivananda Ashram at Haridvar in 1943. The Bihar School of Yoga teaches both householders and renunciates, and has programmes of research on the treatment of mental and physical ailments. Its main centre is the Ganga Darshan Yogashram at Munger, which is in the state of Bihar (another branch is at Rikhia in the state of Jharkhand). In this school, those who wish to participate in the full training programme, which is quite rigorous, are usually required to shave their heads and adopt the orange/brown cloth of the renunciate. The traditional philosophy of yoga and Vedanta is supplemented with a significant component of Tantric philosophy and physiology. The Satyananda system is also called Integral Yoga (which should not be confused with the Integral Yoga of Sri Aurobindo, which is a different system, based primarily on meditation.) Satyananda and his disciple Niranjanananda have published many articles and books on yoga, Tantra and Indian philosophy.

(ix) Other schools of yoga
During the twentieth century, many other yoga institutions were founded, in nearly all instances having a founding guru. They teach meditation and yoga techniques such as those outlined in this article. Most of the larger schools that teach a significant component of postural yoga have been mentioned. However, there are now hundreds of schools all over the world that teach yoga of one form or another, many of them having meditation as a central practice. Among those which are perhaps better known are: the Santa Cruz Yoga Institute, Kaivalyadhama (at Lonavala), the Himalaya Institute (from Svami Rama), the Brahma Kumaris, Sahaja Yoga (from Shri Mataji Nirmala Devi), Kriya Yoga (from Babaji, Shri Yukteshvar, Yogananda and Hariharanda), TM (from Maharishi Mahesh Yogi), Sri Chinmoy, Integral Yoga (Satchidananda), and Siddha Yoga (Muktananda).

References

(1) McEvilley, Thomas (2002). *The Shape of Ancient Thought: Comparative Studies in Greek and Indian Philosophies.* New York: Allworth Press, pp. 219–20.
(2) Translation from *The Upanisads* (ed. and trans. Valerie J. Roebuck), Penguin Books (2003).
(3) Bühnemann (2007), p. 6.
(4) See, for example, Feuerstein (1989), p. 17.
(5) Grönbold (1996).

Bibliography

Ackers, Brian Dana (ed. and trans.) (2002). *The Hatha Yoga Pradipika [by Svatmarama].* Woodstock, New York: YogaVidya.com.

Alter, Joseph S. (2004). *Yoga in Modern India: The Body Between Science and Philosophy.* Oxford/Princeton: Princeton University Press.

Bühnemann, Gudrun (2007). *Eighty-Four Āsanas in Yoga: A Survey of Traditions (with Illustrations).* New Delhi: D. K. Printworld (P) Ltd.

Burley, Mikel (2007). *Classical Sāṃkhya and Yoga: An Indian Metaphysics of Experience.* London/New York: Routledge.

Connolly, Peter (2007). *A Student's Guide to the History and Philosophy of Yoga.* London/Oakville: Equinox Press.

Eliade, Mircea (1990). *Yoga, Immortality and Feeedom.* Princeton: Princeton University Press.

Feuerstein, Georg (1989). *The Yoga-Sūtra of Patañjali (A New Translation and Commentary).* Rochester, Vermont: Inner Traditions International.

Grönbold, Günter (trans. Robert L. Hütwohl) (1996). *The Yoga of Six Limbs: An Introduction to the History of Ṣaḍaṅgayoga.* Santa Fe, New Mexico: Spirit of the Sun Publications.

Iyengar, B. K. S. (1992). *Light on Yoga*. New Delhi: HarperCollins India.

Mallinson, James (2007). *The Khecarīvidyā of Ādinātha (A critical edition and annotated translation of an early text of haṭhayoga)*. London/New York: Routledge.

_____ (ed. and trans.) (2007). *The Shiva Samhita*. Woodstock, New York: YogaVidya.com.

_____ (ed. and trans.) (2004). *The Gheranda Samhita*. Woodstock, New York: YogaVidya.com.

Michelis, Elizabeth De (2004). *A History of Modern Yoga: Patañjali and Western Esotericism*. London/New York: Continuum.

Singleton, Mark (2010). *Yoga Body: The Origins of Modern Yoga Practice*. Oxford/New York: Oxford University Press.

Sjoman, N. E. (1996) *The Yoga Tradition of the Mysore Palace*. New Delhi: Abhinav Publications.

Vasudeva, Somadeva (ed. and trans.) (2004). *The Yoga of the Mālinīvijayottaratantra*. Pondicherry: Institut Français de Pondichéry/École française d'Extrême-Orient.

Verenne, Jean (ed. and trans.) (1971). *Upanishads du Yoga*. Paris: Gallimard.

Whicher, Ian (1998). *The Integrity of the Yoga Darśana: A Reconsideration of Classical Yoga*. Albany: State University of New York Press.

White, David Gordon (2009). *Sinister Yogis*. London/Chicago: University of Chicago Press.

Appendix
Patañjali's Aṣṭāṅga Yoga
(résumé of main concepts)

*Aṣṭāṅga*s (the eight limbs):
External limbs:
    1. *yama* ('restraints'), **2.** *niyama* ('observances'),
    3. *āsana* ('posture'), **4.** *prāṇāyāma* ('breath control'),
    5. *pratyāhāra* ('withdrawal of senses').
Internal limbs [= *saṃyama yoga* (the 'yoga of self-control')]:
    6. *dhāraṇa* ('concentration on an object'),
    7. *dhyāna* ('meditation'),
    8. *samādhi* ('trance') [of two kinds:
    (i). *saṃprajñāta samādhi*
        ('cognitive trance'/'concentration'/'enstasy'),
    (ii). *asaṃprajñāta samādhi*
        ('para-cognitive trance'/'concentration'/'enstasy')].
*Yama*s ('restraints'):
    1. *ahiṃsā* ('non-violence'), 2. *satya* ('truth'),
    3. *asteya* ('non-stealing'), 4. *brahmacārī* ('celibacy'),
    5. *aparigraha* ('non-greed').
*Niyama*s ('observances'):
    1. *śauca* ('cleanliness'), 2. *saṃtoṣa* ('contentment'),
    3. *tapas* ('austerities'), 4. *svādhyāya* ('study on one's own'
        [traditionally, of the *Veda*]),
    5. *īśvarapraṇidhāna* ('concentration on the Lord').
*Kleśa*s ('causes of affliction'):
    1. *avidyā* ('ignorance'), 2. *asmitā* ('egoity'/'one's self'),
    3. *rāga* ('excitement'), 4. *dveṣa* ('aversion'),
    5. *abhiniveṣa* ('perseverance'/'will to live').

*Cittavṛtti*s ('causes of thought'/'movements of the mind'):

    1. *pramāṇa* ('correct conception')
       [*pratyakṣa* ('perception'), *anumāna* ('inference'),
       āgama ('induction')],

    2. *viparyaya* ('incorrect conception'),

    3. *vikalpa* ('doubt'/'uncertainty'),

    4. *nidra* ('sleep'),

    5. *smṛti* ('memory').

Krīyā-yoga:

    1. *tapas* ('raising heat through privations or austerities'),

    2. *svādhyāya*
       ('study on one's own' [traditionally, of the *Veda*s]),

    3. *īśvra-praṇidhāna* ('devotion to the Lord').

Virtues:

    1. *maitrī* ('friendliness'),

    2. *karuṇā* ('compassion'),

    3. *muditā* ('cheerfulness'),

    4. *upekṣa* ('indifference').

Essential practices:

    1. *abhyāsa* ('continuous practice'),

    2. *vairāgya* ('disengagement from the world').

2289092R00017

Printed in Great Britain
by Amazon.co.uk, Ltd.,
Marston Gate.